UNSEEN SCIENCE

What Is Heat?

Laura L. Sullivan

Cavendish Square

New York

Published in 2016 by Cavendish Square Publishing, LLC
243 5th Avenue, Suite 136, New York, NY 10016

Library of Congress Cataloging-in-Publication Data

Sullivan, Laura L. (Laura Lee), author.
What is heat? / Laura L. Sullivan.
pages cm — (Unseen science)
Includes index.
ISBN 978-1-5026-0912-0 (hardcover) ISBN 978-1-5026-0910-6 (paperback) ISBN 978-1-5026-0913-7 (ebook)
1. Heat—Juvenile literature. I. Title. II. Series: Unseen science.
QC256.S83 2016
536—dc23

2015022177

Editorial Director: David McNamara
Editor: Andrew Coddington
Copy Editor: Rebecca Rohan
Art Director: Jeffrey Talbot
Designer: Joseph Macri/Amy Greenan
Senior Production Manager: Jennifer Ryder-Talbot
Production Editor: Renni Johnson
Photo Research: J8 Media

The photographs in this book are used by permission and through the courtesy of: nano/E+/Getty Images, cover; DmitriMaruta/Shutterstock.com, 5; AGorohov/Shutterstock.com, 6; Gary S Chapman/Getty Images, 7; David Crunelle/EyeEm/Getty Images, 8; BlueRingMedia/Shutterstock.com, 9; Luciano Cosmo/Shutterstock.com, 10; Steven Coling/Shutterstock.com, 13; © B.A.E. Inc./Alamy, 14; eyewave/iStock/thinkstock, 15; David Chasey/Getty Images, 15; Ivica Drusany/Shutterstock.com, 16; Innershadows Photography/Shutterstock.com, 18; Pollapat Chirawong/Shutterstock.com. 19; Esteban De Armas/Shutterstock.com, 21; Universal History Archive/UIG via Getty Images, 22; aurielaki/Shutterstock.com, 23; Thomas Koehler/Photothek/Getty Images, 24; trekandshoot/Shutterstock.com, 25.

Printed in the United States of America

CONTENTS

CHAPTER 1

Understanding Heat

On a basic level, you already know what **heat** is. If you step into a bath, you can tell if the water is hot. If you have a fever, your body feels hot. A sunny summer day is hot.

In **physics**, heat is defined as the ability of something to **transfer thermal energy** to other things. Thermal energy and heat are very similar ideas. Thermal energy is inside an object. Heat is the thermal energy that is moved from one object to another. So heat is not so much about what **temperature** an object is, but rather about its ability to spread its energy to another object.

What Is Heat?

People learn about the idea of heat at a very young age. What they are actually learning about is temperature.

Heat or Temperature?

Heat is different than temperature. Temperature is a measure of how hot or cold something is based on a scale. For example, temperature may be measured in degrees Fahrenheit. On the Fahrenheit scale, water starts to boil at 212 degrees Fahrenheit, and freezes at 32 degrees Fahrenheit. Celsius is another temperature

C **F**

50 — 120

40 — 100

30 — 80

20 — 60

10 — 40

0 —

10 — 20

20 — 0

scale. On that system of measurement, water boils at 100 degrees Celsius, and freezes at zero degrees Celsius. Temperature is measured with a **thermometer**.

Heat is a kind of **energy**. All things are made up of tiny components called **molecules**. These molecules are always **vibrating**. As the temperature rises, the molecules vibrate faster. This increase in movement is the object's thermal energy. The hotter the temperature, the more movement there is. The more movement there is, the more energy is present.

Thermal Energy

This transfer of heat, or thermal energy, can be seen in everyday life. If you run a hot bath and leave the water in the tub long enough, the water will cool. The hot water will transfer some of its energy to

Mass, or how big something is, can affect its thermal energy. A cool pool has more thermal energy than a hot drink because it is much bigger.

the air, and to the tub. Eventually, the water will be about the same temperature as the things around it. Its heat energy has moved.

Thermal energy doesn't just depend on temperature, though. A cold swimming pool actually has more thermal energy than a hot cup of cocoa. The cocoa might have a much higher temperature, but it is very small. The pool is colder than the cocoa, but it is much, much bigger. There are many more molecules vibrating in the swimming pool. Therefore, it has greater thermal energy than the cup of cocoa.

How Heat Moves

Heat can transfer in three ways: **conduction**, **convection**, and **radiation**. Heat is moved to **solid** things by conduction. If you use a spoon to stir your hot cocoa, the rapidly vibrating molecules of the hot cocoa make the molecules at the bottom of the spoon vibrate more quickly. Those molecules bump into other molecules in the spoon, making them move faster, too. So even if the handle of the spoon isn't in the cocoa, it becomes hot, too, by conduction.

Heat moves in **liquids** or **gases** by convection. Hot molecules in liquids or gases can move more freely than in solids. When hot, fast-moving molecules move farther apart, they make space for colder, slower-

Heat is transferred through solids by the process of conduction. Quickly vibrating molecules bump against other nearby molecules, causing them to vibrate more quickly, too.

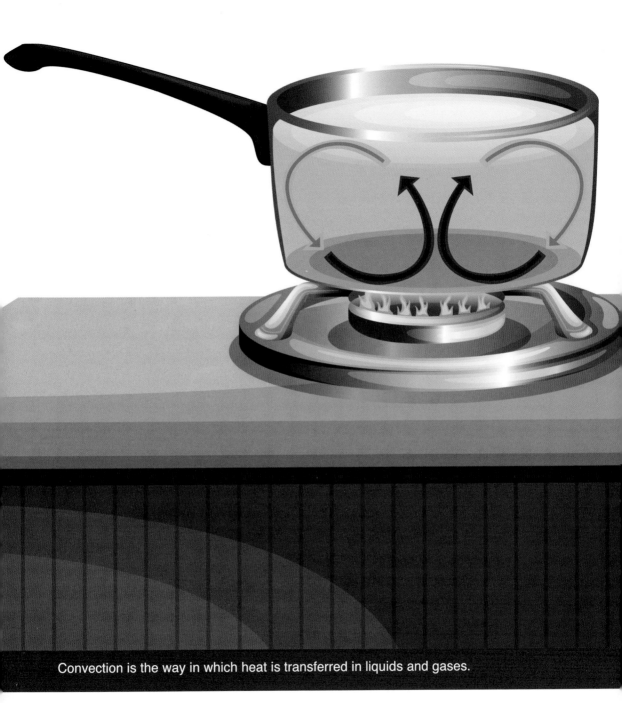

Convection is the way in which heat is transferred in liquids and gases.

moving molecules. Heat is then transferred from hot to cold places by convection.

Radiation is the transfer of energy as waves. Those waves can travel through places with little or no molecules, like space. The sun transfers heat to Earth through radiation. Even though the sun is about 93 million miles (150 million kilometers) away from Earth, we can still feel its heat.

This Chapter Has Shown

Heat is the ability of something to transfer thermal energy to something else. Heat is a kind of energy. All molecules vibrate. When there is more heat, molecules vibrate faster. Heat can be transferred by conduction, convection, or radiation.

The sun's heat is transferred to Earth (and into the rest of space) by radiation. It takes about eight minutes for heat to travel from the sun to Earth.

CHAPTER 2

Experiment with Heat

There are many ways to study the effects of heat at home or school. Since heat **experiments** involve hot things, have a parent, teacher, or other responsible adult help you.

Objective

Perform a two-part experiment that shows 1) the difference in thermal energy between large and small amounts of water, and 2) the process of conduction.

Materials

- A stove
- A large pot
- A small pot

A small pot of water starts to boil much more quickly than a large pot containint more water.

- A timer
- A kitchen thermometer
- Several spoons or similar kitchen tools made of different materials (plastic, wood, silicone, metal, etc.)

Procedure

1. Fill the small pot and the large pot with water. Then, have an adult put them on the stove and turn the settings of both burners to high.

2. Set a timer and see how long it takes each pot to boil. Note your results.

3. Have an adult take the pots off the stove and place them in a safe place. Using a candy thermometer or other cooking thermometer, carefully test the temperature of each pot of water. Test both of them again every few minutes and write down your results.

Hot water left at room temperature will eventually cool down to about the temperature of the air. Ice water will also eventually reach room temperature.

A large amount of water takes longer to boil, but afterward it stays hot much longer than a small amount of water.

By putting spoons made from different materials into hot water, you can see how conduction works, and also test to find out which materials are the best conductors.

4. When you have gathered your data, have an adult reheat the large pot of water. It does not have to boil, but it should be quite hot.

5. Place the different kinds of spoons in the water. The rounded end of the spoon should be in the water.

What Is Heat?

The handle should be out of the water. Make sure the different utensils don't touch each other.

6. Carefully touch the handle of each spoon. Note your discoveries. Feel them again every minute, but stop if they get too hot.

Questions

- Which boils faster, a large quantity of water, or a small quantity of water?
- Which cools faster?
- In the spoon experiment, do the handles feel like they are different temperatures? Which materials get hotter faster? Which spoons take longer to warm up?
- Why might you want something to be made out of a material that doesn't conduct heat well—or something that conducts heat very well? Think about pot holders to protect hands, or pans that help cook food faster.

Cooks and bakers might use metal equipment because metal is a good conductor. It transfers heat well, so food cooks quickly and evenly.

Conclusion

Even though both pots have equal heat under them, the smaller amount of water will boil much faster than the large amount of water. However, you will find that the larger amount of water stays hotter for longer. Although they were both heated to the same temperature, the larger quantity of water has greater thermal energy. Eventually, though, both will reach room temperature.

Conduction is the way in which heat is transferred from one molecule to its neighbor. Some materials conduct heat better than others. In the spoon experiment, some of the materials heated up quickly. The metal spoon probably heated up the fastest. Metal is a

A pan of hot water has a lot of thermal energy. That energy can be used to cook food, such as hardboiled eggs.

good conductor. The spoons that took longer to warm up are made from materials that don't conduct heat very well, such as wood or silicone.

These properties are useful to know about when working in the kitchen. A pot holder, for example, should be a poor conductor. When you use it to pick up a hot pot, you want the heat to transfer very slowly. That way your hand won't get burned. But when you want to cook something quickly, pick a pot or pan made out of a good conductor, like metal. That way it will reach the desired temperature faster and help the food cook more quickly.

CHAPTER 3

Heat in Daily Life

Heat was one of the earliest physical sciences that our ancestors explored. Fire is a way to generate heat. Early humans might have first used fire more than one million years ago. By about one hundred thousand years ago, people were using fire to provide light and warmth, and to cook food. Cooking food is a kind of heat transfer. When food is heated, its structure and temperature changes. Heat often makes food easier to chew and digest. Heating food can also destroy dangerous organisms that might make people sick.

Early humans learned to use fire as a source of both heat and light. Cooking was an early use of heat conduction.

Steam Power from Heat

Humans learned how to turn heat energy into mechanical energy. In other words, they made heat do work for them. One of the basic ways to make heat do work is by creating steam. When water is boiled, it turns from a liquid to a gas. The gas is called steam. The pressure of the steam can actually push moving parts.

Steam generated from heat was used to power engines in the eighteenth and nineteenth centuries. Early steam engines were used in factories. In 1804, the first steam-driven train ran in Britain. Steamships became common on rivers and seas shortly afterward.

Electricity from Heat

Heat is the primary source of most electricity that we use today. In a coal-fueled power plant, the coal is burned to heat water, creating steam. That steam spins a turbine that moves a magnet around a wire. That makes a magnetic field that sends a current of electricity through the wire. In other power plants, heat might be made by burning natural gas. In a nuclear power plant, heat is created by splitting uranium atoms.

The steam produced from heat powers a turbine, which generates an electrical current, which eventually travels to your house in the form of electricity.

Heat Energy from the Sun

The sun provides an incredible abundance of heat that can be harnessed for energy. Many solar power devices focus on **photovoltaics**, or using the sun's light to produce energy. Other systems, though, make use of the sun's heat.

There are three main kinds of **solar thermal collectors**. Low-temperature collectors use flat plates to collect the sun's heat.

Heat from the sun can be used to heat water for household use or swimming pools.

They are often used for heating swimming pools. Household water and air can be heated with medium-temperature collectors. These systems also use flat plates.

High-temperature collectors are used for generating electricity at some power plants. The Ivanpah Solar Electric Generating System, located in California's Mojave Desert, is the world's largest concentrated solar thermal plant. It uses huge mirrors to focus solar heat on boilers.

Solar thermal energy is a way to get clean, renewable energy. Burning coal creates **greenhouse gases** that contribute to **climate change**. Someday, the world will run out of coal and other fossil

What Is Heat?

fuels. But the sun will continue to produce light and heat for a few billion more years. As technologies develop, we can make greater use of both the sun's light and heat.

This Chapter Has Shown

People have been making heat work for them for thousands of years. Fires were used for cooking. Later, heat made steam that was used for mechanical energy. It powered ships and trains. Today, heat is converted into electricity in power plants. The heat from the sun can also be harvested for human needs.

The Ivanpah Solar Electric Generating System uses the sun's heat to make electricity. It reduces carbon dioxide emissions by about 400,000 tons per year.

GLOSSARY

climate change Alteration of global or regional weather patterns, particularly due to human-related activities such as burning fossil fuels.

conduction The way in which heat or electricity passes through a solid.

convection The way in which heat is transferred in a liquid or gas.

energy The ability to do work; energy can be in many forms including heat, light, electricity, or kinetic (movement).

experiment A scientific process done to test an idea or prove a fact.

gas A state of matter without a fixed shape, in which molecules expand to fill available space.

greenhouse gases Gases that absorb infrared radiation and contribute to the greenhouse effect, influencing climate change.

heat The ability of something to transfer thermal energy to something else.

liquid A state of matter in which molecules move to take the shape of their container.

molecule The smallest unit of a chemical, made up of bonded atoms.

photovoltaics The science or technology of turning sunlight into energy.

physics The branch of science that studies matter and energy.

radiation Energy that is transmitted in rays or waves, such as light or heat energy from the sun.

solar thermal collector A device that produces energy by gathering heat from the sun.

GLOSSARY

solid A state of matter in which the molecules are in fixed positions.

temperature The relative degree of heat as measured by a particular scale, such as Fahrenheit or Celsius.

thermal energy The energy present in an object due to the vibration of its molecules.

thermometer A device used for measuring temperature.

transfer To move something from one place to another.

vibrate To move or quiver rapidly back and forth.

What Is Heat?

Books

Sneidman, Joshua and Erin Twamley. *Climate Change: Discover How It Impacts Spaceship Earth*. White River Junction, VT: Nomad Press, 2015.

Stille, Darlene R. *Heat*. Chicago: Heinemann-Raintree, 2012.

Thomas, Isabel. *Experiments with Heating and Cooling*. Chicago: Heinemann-Raintree, 2015.

Websites

Physics Central

www.physicscentral.com

With physics information for all ages and interest levels, this site also has an Ask-a-Physicist section.

FIND OUT MORE

Physics4Kids

www.physics4kids.com

This site covers many aspects of physics in an easy-to-understand way.

Science Kids: Physics

www.sciencekids.co.nz/physics.html

This New Zealand—based site has pages on all aspects of science, including physics experiments to try at home.

INDEX

Page numbers in **boldface** are illustrations. Entries in **boldface** are glossary terms.

Laura L. Sullivan is the author of more than thirty fiction and nonfiction books for children, including the fantasies *Under the Green Hill* and *Guardian of the Green Hill*. She has written many books for Cavendish Square, including two others in the Unseen Science series: *What Is Gravity?* and *What Is Motion?*